OCCASIONAL
PAPER

# Regulating Older Drivers

## Are New Policies Needed?

David S. Loughran, Seth A. Seabury,
Laura Zakaras

RAND INSTITUTE FOR CIVIL JUSTICE

The research described in this report was conducted by the RAND Institute for Civil Justice.

**Library of Congress Cataloging-in-Publication Data**

Loughran, David S., 1969-
    Regulating older drivers : are new policies needed? / David S. Loughran, Seth A. Seabury, Laura Zakaras.
       p. cm.
    Includes bibliographical references.
    ISBN 978-0-8330-4194-4 (pbk. : alk. paper)
    1. Drivers' licenses—United States. 2. Older automobile drivers—Government policy—United States.
3. Traffic safety—United States—Evaluation. 4. Risk assessment—United States. 5. Traffic regulations—
United States.  I. Seabury, Seth A. II. Zakaras, Laura. III. Title.

KF2218.L68 2007
343.7309'46—dc22

                                                                          2007026181

The RAND Corporation is a nonprofit research organization providing objective analysis and effective solutions that address the challenges facing the public and private sectors around the world. RAND's publications do not necessarily reflect the opinions of its research clients and sponsors.

**RAND®** is a registered trademark.

Published 2007 by the RAND Corporation
1776 Main Street, P.O. Box 2138, Santa Monica, CA 90407-2138
1200 South Hayes Street, Arlington, VA 22202-5050
4570 Fifth Avenue, Suite 600, Pittsburgh, PA 15213-2665
RAND URL: http://www.rand.org/
To order RAND documents or to obtain additional information, contact
Distribution Services: Telephone: (310) 451-7002;
Fax: (310) 451-6915; Email: order@rand.org

# Preface

Policymakers, insurers, and the public have long been concerned about the effects of aging on the ability to operate a motor vehicle safely. Under the assumption that older drivers are more dangerous than are younger drivers, many states impose stricter licensing requirements on older drivers. As the proportion of licensed drivers 65 and older continues to increase, states may impose additional licensing requirements on older drivers in an attempt to lessen the threat that older drivers pose to traffic safety.

This paper presents new evidence on the threat that older drivers pose to traffic safety and discusses what this new evidence implies for public policy. It draws on recent RAND research that employs an innovative statistical procedure to estimate the relative risk posed by older drivers, as detailed in the technical report, *Estimating the Accident Risk of Older Drivers* (Loughran and Seabury, 2007). This paper summarizes the findings and policy implications of that study for policy audiences, including the insurance industry, public agencies, and other organizations concerned about driver safety and the welfare of older Americans. This paper was written with support from the RAND Institute for Civil Justice (ICJ).

## The RAND Institute for Civil Justice

The mission of ICJ is to improve private and public decisionmaking on civil legal issues by supplying policymakers and the public with the results of objective, empirically based, analytic research. ICJ facilitates change in the civil justice system by analyzing trends and outcomes, identifying and evaluating policy options, and bringing together representatives of different interests to debate alternative solutions to policy problems. ICJ builds on a long tradition of RAND research characterized by an interdisciplinary, empirical approach to public policy issues and rigorous standards of quality, objectivity, and independence.

ICJ research is supported by pooled grants from corporations, trade and professional associations, and individuals; by government grants and contracts; and by private foundations. ICJ disseminates its work widely to the legal, business, and research communities and to the general public. In accordance with RAND policy, all ICJ research products are subject to peer review before publication. ICJ publications do not necessarily reflect the opinions or policies of the research sponsors or of the ICJ Board of Overseers.

Information about ICJ is available online (http://www.rand.org/icj). Inquiries about research projects should be sent to the following address:

Robert T. Reville, Director
RAND Institute for Civil Justice
1776 Main Street
P.O. Box 2138
Santa Monica, CA 90407-2138
310-393-0411 x6786
Fax: 310-451-6979
Robert_Reville@rand.org

# Contents

# Figures

# Tables

# Acknowledgments

This paper has benefited from the contributions of many colleagues both inside and outside of RAND. We are particularly grateful to Christopher Nelson of RAND, who formally reviewed this paper. We are also grateful to Greg Ridgeway, also of RAND, and David Grabowski of Harvard Medical School, who reviewed the supporting technical report. We also thank attendees of the ICJ brown-bag series; members of the ICJ Insurance Advisory Committee and the ICJ board of overseers for their helpful comments on earlier presentations of this work; Carole Roan Gresenz, the ICJ quality-assurance coordinator; and Robert Reville, director of ICJ, for their early support of this research and constructive guidance throughout the course of the project. Finally, we thank Patricia McClure for her excellent research assistance.

# Abbreviations

FARS      Fatal Accident Reporting System

GES      General Estimates System

NHTS      National Household Transportation Survey

PD      property damage

VMT      vehicle miles traveled

# CHAPTER ONE

# Introduction

In July 2003, an 86-year-old man drove his 1982 Buick into a crowd of pedestrians shopping at an open-air farmers' market in Santa Monica, California, killing 10 and injuring more than 50. In October 2005, a 93-year-old man struck a pedestrian in St. Petersburg, Florida, and did not notice the corpse hanging out his windshield until a tollbooth operator stopped him ("National Briefing," 2005). Shocking incidents such as these have reinvigorated a long-simmering debate over the riskiness of older drivers and led to calls for stricter state licensing policies for these drivers.[1] The issue is particularly important in light of demographic projections: By 2025, drivers 65 and older will represent 25 percent of the driving population, compared to 15 percent in 2001.

Although it has been scientifically established that physical and cognitive degeneration at older ages compromises driving ability, it is not clear just how much riskier older drivers are than other drivers. Most published research shows that accidents per mile driven increase when drivers are in their fifties and, by the time they reach their eighties, accidents per mile driven are almost as high as they are for the youngest drivers (see, for example, Li, Braver, and Chen, 2003). As we describe later, however, this measure of risk can be misleading.

Our research departs from previous studies that rely on this measure. Instead, we use an innovative statistical method to estimate the likelihood that older drivers will cause an accident relative to the likelihood that other drivers will cause an accident, controlling for vehicle miles driven. We will refer to this statistic throughout this paper as the *relative riskiness* of older drivers. Levitt and Porter (2001) first devised and employed our statistical method in their study of the relative riskiness of drunk drivers. Based on our findings, we make a number of policy recommendations aimed at stemming the rise in traffic-related injuries and deaths that are expected as the average age of the driving population increases.

---

[1] See, for example, the op-ed "A Crash Course for the Elderly" in the *New York Times*:

> In July 2003, an 86-year-old driver plowed through a crowd in Santa Monica, Calif., killing 10 and injuring dozens. Yet . . . three years and many tragedies later, . . . nothing has been done to prevent this recurring nightmare. . . . We should require continuing education for all drivers and licensing recertification and mandatory road testing for drivers age 65 and older. It would make the roads safer for all. (Haas, 2006)

Also see "Wrong Way" (2007), which advocates road tests for drivers 75 and older.

## Background

Medical research has demonstrated that, as people age, their driving ability becomes impaired. The most common problem is declining eyesight: Glaucoma, macular degeneration, and cataracts—all of which become more common with age—reduce night and peripheral vision and vision acuity and cause individuals to become more sensitive to glare (Voelker, 1999). Impaired vision is strongly associated with a greater likelihood of causing an accident among older drivers (Ball et al., 2005). Normal changes in brain functioning slow reflex reactions and reduce the ability to take in information from disparate sources simultaneously (Ponds, Brouwer, and Van Wolffelaar, 1988). Severer changes in brain functioning, such as depression and dementia, as well as the medications used to treat those illnesses, may seriously hamper an older person's ability to drive. Other common afflictions of older people—heart disease, arthritis, and insomnia, for example—can also reduce driving skills.

There is also evidence, however, that older individuals compensate for their impairment by changing their driving behavior. Many older drivers drive less frequently, and, when they do drive, they tend to avoid high-speed zones and driving at night (Baldock et al., 2006; Vance et al., 2006; Stutts, 1998; Jorgensen and Polak, 1993; Kington et al., 1993; Foley et al., 2002; Marottoli et al., 1993). Eventually, most older individuals decide to stop driving altogether, either because they recognize that they are likelier to cause an accident or because a family member or doctor urges them to stop driving. To identify the appropriate policy response to older drivers, such self-regulation must be taken into account.

Many states have already responded to the perceived risk posed by older drivers by creating stiffer licensing requirements as drivers age. Some states require older drivers to renew their licenses in person and with greater frequency than younger drivers and to pass vision tests at renewal. Fewer states require older drivers to pass written tests and require older drivers to take road tests.[2] Should more DMVs adopt road tests for older individuals or, as AARP recommends, generally devote more resources to screening older drivers for competency and provide remedial training and education to those who need it?[3]

## Study Purpose and Approach

To inform the policy debate surrounding older drivers, our study sought to answer four related questions:

- How much likelier are older drivers than other drivers to cause a crash?
- How much less do older drivers drive than other drivers do?

---

[2]   For more about state-level licensing policies that target older drivers, see IIHS (2007) and III (2007).

[3]   See AARP (2006, Chapter Nine, p. 7): "Federal, state and local governments should support the expansion of programs and the number of qualified professionals performing scientifically based driver assessment, rehabilitation, and education."

- How much more vulnerable are they than other drivers to being injured or killed in accidents?
- To what extent do older drivers take steps on their own to mitigate the risks of driving?

At first glance, it might seem straightforward to answer the first question. All that appears to be needed is to divide the number of automobile accidents caused by drivers of different age groups by a measure of their prevalence on the road, such as miles driven. However, the data on accidents, their cause, and average miles traveled for different age groups are unreliable, as we explain in Chapter Two. Another approach had to be developed.

We employed a statistical method first developed by Levitt and Porter (2001) to estimate the riskiness of drunk drivers relative to sober drivers. Using the Fatal Accident Reporting System (FARS), which provides high-quality data on all fatal crashes recorded since 1975, Levitt and Porter analyzed two-car fatal accidents involving drunk and sober drivers. For our purposes, we examined two-car crashes between pairs of drivers from three age groups: younger drivers (15 to 24 years old), adult drivers (25 to 64 years old), and older drivers (65 and older). Knowing the age group of the driver of each car in two-car fatal crashes (e.g., two older drivers, two adult drivers, one adult driver and one older driver), we could estimate the relative riskiness of older drivers, the relative amount they drive (to which we refer as their *relative exposure*), and their relative likelihood of being killed in a car accident (to which we refer as their *relative fragility*). We offer more detail about our methods in Chapter Two.

We found that drivers 65 and older are slightly likelier (specifically, 16 percent likelier) than adult drivers to cause an accident. Young drivers, on the other hand, are 188 percent likelier than adult drivers to cause an accident. We also found that older drivers and their passengers are nearly seven times likelier than adult drivers and their passengers to be killed in an accident. This could help explain why, despite medical evidence that suggests that driving ability should decline with age, the older individuals who do drive are not much more dangerous than middle-aged drivers. Because older drivers pose such a large risk to themselves, the riskiest older drivers choose to curtail their driving the most, leaving safer older drivers on the road.

Coverage of the older-driver issue in the popular press has largely focused on the very oldest drivers (e.g., 75 and older) (see, for example, Davis and DeBarros, 2007). While we find that drivers 70 and older are no riskier than drivers 65 and older, we are unable to examine with our methods the riskiness of the very oldest drivers. We note, however, that, while riskiness may increase at such advanced ages, there are very few of these drivers on the road, so their overall contribution to accident rates is likely to be small.

Altogether, these findings suggest that state DMVs should carefully weigh the costs and benefits of imposing stricter licensing requirements on older drivers. On the one hand, requiring older drivers to take road tests, for example, would certainly identify some older drivers whose driving abilities have deteriorated unacceptably. But our results suggest that there are relatively few older drivers who need to be legally prohibited from driving, so these drivers pose a relatively small risk to traffic safety overall. And the costs of requiring all older drivers to take such a test are not insignificant, either in terms of staffing resources or in terms of the stigma that older drivers might experience as a result of being singled out solely on the basis of age.

Nonetheless, automobile travel is clearly dangerous for older drivers and passengers because they are more susceptible to injury. Policies that promote safer automobile design, offer alternatives to automobile travel, and reduce the riskiness of younger drivers (who are far likelier to cause an accident both because they are riskier and because they drive more) could help stem the rise in injuries and fatalities that is likely to occur with an aging population.

## Organization of This Paper

This paper is intended to summarize previously published research in terms that will make it accessible to public and private decisionmakers concerned about driver safety and the welfare of older Americans. Chapter Two summarizes the methods we used to perform the analysis, described in detail in a separate report (Loughran and Seabury, 2007). Chapter Three presents what we found about the relative riskiness of older drivers, their relative exposure, their relative fragility, and how they adjust their driving habits as they age. In Chapter Four, we explore the policy implications of these results.

# Estimating the Relative Riskiness of Older Drivers

A commonly employed measure of riskiness is accidents divided by vehicle miles traveled (VMT). This statistic provides a measure of the frequency with which drivers are involved in accidents. Importantly, it accounts for how many miles drivers drive, which varies across age groups of drivers. Older drivers, for example, drive fewer miles on average than do younger drivers.

The data needed to compute this statistic are readily available. Data on accidents can be obtained from the U.S. Department of Transportation's General Estimates System (GES), which annually records the characteristics of a nationally representative probability sample of accidents reported to the police. Data on VMT are available in the National Household Transportation Survey (NHTS), a nationally representative sample of U.S. households asked to record miles driven during the preceding week.

In Figure 2.1, we graph accidents divided by VMT by age, using data from GES and the 2001 NHTS. Figure 2.1 normalizes the accident-to-VMT ratio to 1.0 for the age group of drivers with the lowest accident-to-VMT ratio, drivers 60 to 64 years old. Thus, Figure 2.1 shows accident rates relative to drivers 60 to 64 years old. As shown, both younger and older drivers are at elevated risk of being in an accident. Younger drivers are nearly three times as likely to be involved in an accident per VMT as drivers 60 to 64 years old. By this measure, the relative riskiness of drivers declines with age until ages 60 to 64 and then begins to increase. Drivers 85 and older are nearly as risky as the youngest drivers. Their relative risk of being in an accident is about 3.4 times that of drivers 60 to 64 years old.

However, there are problems with the accident and VMT data that make us question whether Figure 2.1 provides an accurate picture of how relative riskiness varies with age. First, the GES records only police-reported accidents. Since many accidents are not reported to the police, the GES is likely to greatly underestimate the total number of accidents that occur in the United States each year. Moreover, because police-reported accidents are much likelier to involve an injury than are unreported accidents, these accident numbers are likely to overrepresent accidents involving older drivers.[1] This is because older drivers are much more susceptible than younger drivers to the physical trauma of an accident and so are much likelier to be injured

---

[1] The notion that accidents are likelier to be reported if they involve severer outcomes, such as an injury, has been shown in other contexts (see Mendeloff et al., 2006).

**Figure 2.1**
**Accidents per Mile Driven, by Driver Age**

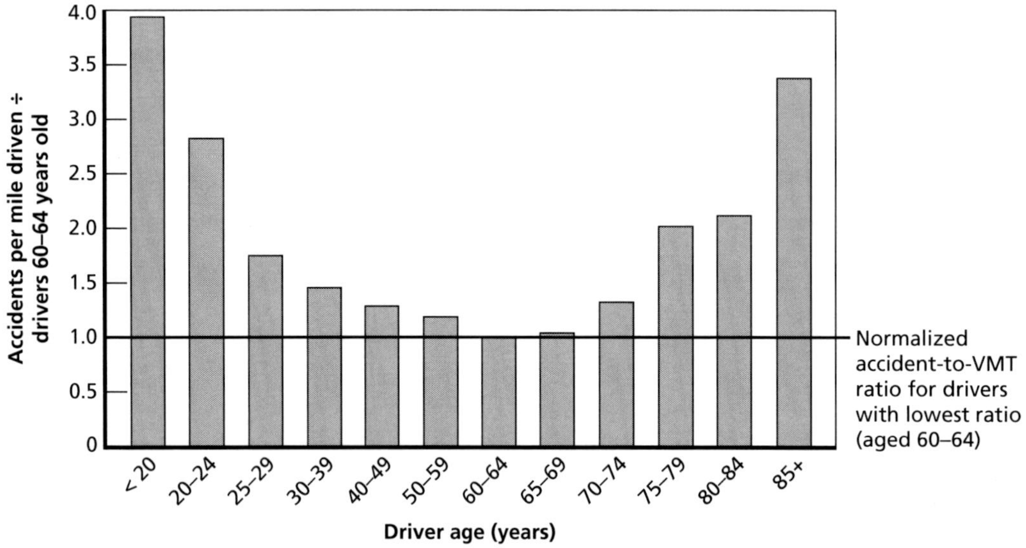

RAND OP189-2.1

(Evans and Gerrish, 2001; Kim et al., 1995; Augenstein, 2001; Li, Braver, and Chen, 2003; Evans, 1988).

Another problem with the accident data is that they do not provide a reliable way of determining who was at fault. Thus, although the data might show that some group of individuals appears to be *involved* in more accidents, we cannot say for certain whether this group in fact *causes* more accidents.

We also are concerned that the data on VMT may be unreliable, since they are derived from surveys that ask respondents to record miles driven for car trips they took during the preceding week. These self-reports likely measure VMT with error, and that error may be correlated with respondent age. For example, older drivers may be more diligent in recording VMT for the purposes of the survey. The precise nature of the error is impossible to know beforehand, but it reduces confidence in the age profile described in Figure 2.1.[2]

The method we employ to estimate the relative riskiness of older drivers, derived from Levitt and Porter (2001), requires data only on fatal accidents. There are three main advantages to our method. First, we need not rely on the GES, which, as we just explained, records information on a potentially nonrepresentative sample of accidents (both fatal and nonfatal). Instead, we employ annual (1975–2003) data from the FARS, which records information on every fatal accident that occurs on public roads in the United States. Second, our approach does not require us to have any information on who caused a particular accident, which can

---

[2]    An alternative measure of riskiness is property damage (PD) claims made against at-fault drivers as a fraction of insured vehicles. PD statistics show a U-shaped pattern similar to that in Figure 2.1 (IIHS, 2003), but there could be reporting problems with these data as well. For example, older drivers may be likelier than other drivers to accept blame for accidents in which they are involved. Older drivers might also be likelier than other drivers to carry insurance.

be difficult to discern. Finally, we do not need any information on how many miles a given group of drivers drives, which allows us to avoid using the self-reported VMT data contained in the NHTS.

Readers might rightly question how we can compute relative riskiness with only data on the number of fatal accidents involving drivers of different ages. Levitt and Porter (2001) liken this to estimating free-throw percentages without knowing how many free throws were attempted. Here, we explain the logic behind our method by way of example. Readers interested in a formal exposition of our method should refer to Loughran and Seabury (2007).

To understand the logic behind our method, it is useful to imagine a stretch of road on which two groups, older drivers and adult drivers, are driving and passing each other (the same logic applies for comparing young drivers to adult drivers). In some cases, two older drivers might crash into each other, a fatality will result, and we will observe a crash in the fatal accident numbers recorded in the FARS. In other cases, two adult drivers might crash into each other, a fatality will result, and we will observe this crash in the data.

Now suppose that we observed 100 of these crashes involving two older drivers and 200 involving two adult drivers. What can we infer about the relative riskiness of older drivers? Suppose that we could assume that adult and older drivers are equally likely to cause a crash. With that assumption, we could infer that adults account for twice as many miles driven, because they are involved in twice as many crashes. On the other hand, if we could assume that adult and older drivers accounted for an equal share of miles driven, we would infer that adults are twice as likely to cause a crash, because twice as many crashes involved adults.

Of course, we cannot make either of those assumptions, so observing the number of two-car fatal crashes between drivers from the same age group (e.g., two older drivers or two adult drivers) alone is not enough for our purposes. With only this information, we cannot separately identify relative riskiness and relative exposure. Note that we would be confronted with the same problem if we focused on one-car crashes.

However, there is a third type of accident, accidents between older and adult drivers, that provides us with the missing information that we need to make inferences about the relative riskiness and relative exposure of older drivers. To see how crashes of this type aid our analysis, consider the three examples illustrated in Table 2.1. In example 1, we observe 100 crashes involving two adult drivers, 100 crashes involving two older drivers, and 200 crashes involving both types of drivers. In this example, 300 total crashes involve adults and 300 total crashes involve older drivers. Moreover, drivers crash into other drivers from a different age group as

**Table 2.1**
**Examples of Numbers of Fatal Crashes Involving Drivers of Different Ages**

| Crash Type | Example 1 | Example 2 | Example 3 |
|---|---|---|---|
| Adult + adult | 100 | 100 | 100 |
| Older + older | 100 | 75 | 125 |
| Adult + older | 200 | 225 | 175 |
| Total | 400 | 400 | 400 |

often as they crash into drivers from the same age group. Thus, we can infer from these numbers that adult and older drivers are equally likely to cause a crash and drive equal amounts.

Now consider example 2. In this example, adult drivers are involved in 325 crashes and older drivers are involved in 300 crashes. This example shows that older drivers crash into other adult drivers more often than they crash into other older drivers (the rate is 225/75, or 3 to 1). Adult drivers also crash into older drivers more frequently than they crash into other adult drivers, but the relative rate at which this happens is less (a rate of 225/100, or 2.25 to 1). Taken together, these facts suggest that adult drivers are more prevalent on the road than older drivers are—either there are more of them or they drive more miles or both—and that older drivers are likelier to make a mistake and cause a crash.

The reverse is true in example 3, in which we observe 125 crashes involving two older drivers and 175 crashes involving an adult and older driver. Now, older drivers are involved in more crashes (300) than are adult drivers (275). And older drivers are crashing into other older drivers more often than they were crashing into adults in examples 1 and 2. Thus, from the numbers presented in example 3, we infer that older drivers are more prevalent on the road and less likely (more precisely, we infer that they are *no likelier*) to cause a crash than are adult drivers.

A considerable amount of additional work is necessary to go from numbers of fatal accidents to precise estimates of relative riskiness and exposure. Since these examples are completely hypothetical, we do not provide actual estimates. The point of the examples is to illustrate how different numbers of crashes involving adult and older drivers provide information about their relative riskiness and exposure. In short, the more frequently older drivers crash into adult drivers relative to the frequency with which they crash into other older drivers, the riskier they are relative to adults. Importantly, these data permit us to make inferences about *relative*, not *absolute*, risk and exposure. For example, if we were to double the number of crashes in each of the rows of Table 2.1, those new numbers would imply the same *relative* riskiness and exposure as implied by the actual numbers in Table 2.1. To compute *absolute* riskiness, we would need to have data on VMT, which do not appear in the FARS.

The Levitt and Porter (2001) method requires us to make a number of assumptions that we detail in Loughran and Seabury (2007). We describe three of the more critical assumptions here. First, we must assume that older drivers, on average, are at least as likely as adult drivers to make a mistake. Of course, there is a wealth of medical evidence to suggest that older drivers have impairments that reduce their driving ability, evidence that provides support for our assumption that they are at least as risky as adult drivers.

The second critical assumption is what Levitt and Porter (2001) refer to as the *equal mixing* assumption: Older and adult drivers encounter each other on the road at rates similar to their rate in the population. If there are twice as many adult as older drivers on the road, for example, then older drivers must encounter adult drivers twice as often as they encounter other older drivers.

To see why this assumption is important, suppose that we had a barrel full of apples and oranges and that we wanted to estimate the fraction of apples by pulling out 20 pieces of fruit and computing the fraction of apples in our sample. If all the apples were poured into the barrel at once and all the oranges were poured in on top of them, we could not accurately estimate this fraction with our 20 pieces of fruit. But, if someone shook the barrel to spread the apples and oranges out so they were equally mixed, then we could. While the assumption of equal mixing probably does not hold for the entire United States, since there are certainly clusters of older and younger drivers across the country, it is much likelier to hold if we focus on very specific combinations of geographic locations and times of day. So, when we estimate relative risk, we do so for these specific "cells," then average across them.

The third critical assumption is that the reasons that a driver makes a mistake that causes a two-car fatal accident are no different from the reasons that that same driver makes a mistake that causes some other kind of accident. This assumption allows us to make inferences about the relative riskiness of older drivers under all circumstances, not just those leading to a two-car fatal accident. We admit that the validity of this assumption is difficult to evaluate. For example, it could be that older drivers are less careful when driving at very low speeds, making them likelier than other drivers to cause a fender-bender, but much more careful when driving at higher speeds, making them less likely than other drivers to cause an injury accident. Since the policy debate focuses largely on the costs that older drivers impose on others in terms of injury rather than minor property damage, these estimates, even if they best apply to serious accidents, are nonetheless relevant.

The Levitt and Porter (2001) method is not specifically designed to address the possibility that drivers in different age groups have different likelihoods of being killed in a crash. Because data only appear in the FARS if someone dies, the increased fragility of older drivers means that a higher portion of their accidents will involve a fatality, which would cause us to overestimate both the relative riskiness and relative exposure of older drivers. However, we were able to correct this bias by estimating the relative fragility of older drivers, then using that estimate to adjust our estimates of the relative riskiness and exposure of older drivers. To estimate the relative fragility of older drivers, we used data on two-car fatal crashes involving one adult and one older driver. By comparing the fatality rate of older and adult drivers in these crashes, we obtain an estimate of the relative fragility of older drivers.

# CHAPTER THREE

# The Relative Riskiness of Older Drivers

The objective of stricter licensing requirements and other policies targeting older drivers is to make the roads safer for all. But, to debate whether such policies are needed, we need to answer the following questions: How much likelier are older drivers than other drivers to cause a crash? How much less do older drivers drive than other drivers do? How much more vulnerable are they than other drivers to being injured or killed in accidents? To what extent do older drivers take steps on their own to mitigate the risks of driving? Our methods allow us to answer the first three questions directly. Our methods do not provide a direct answer to the fourth question, but we can make inferences about the extent and effectiveness of self-regulation by older drivers based on our results. In this chapter, we summarize our findings.

## Findings

### The Relative Riskiness and Exposure of Older Drivers

Our most important finding is that older drivers are not that much riskier than adult drivers and far less risky than young adult drivers. Older drivers are 16 percent likelier to cause a crash than adult drivers are. While that difference is significant, it is perhaps far smaller than the conventional wisdom, fueled by anecdote, would imply that it would be. And it is nowhere near the risk that younger drivers pose to the public. As shown in the first pair of bars in Figure 3.1, the youngest drivers are 188 percent likelier than adult drivers to cause a crash.

We also find that older drivers drive far less than adult drivers do. The second pair of bars in Figure 3.1 shows that, on average, older drivers drive 38 percent fewer miles than do adult drivers. Younger drivers, on the other hand, drive about 54 percent more miles than adult drivers do.

Together, these findings suggest that younger drivers pose a much greater risk to traffic safety than do older drivers, both because they are likelier to cause a crash and because they drive many more miles. By our estimates, older drivers, who represent 15 percent of all licensed drivers, cause 7 percent of all two-car accidents (both fatal and nonfatal). Younger drivers, on the other hand, who represent 13 percent of all licensed drivers, cause 43 percent of all two-car accidents.

**Figure 3.1**
**The Relative Riskiness, Exposure, and Fragility of Older and Younger Drivers**

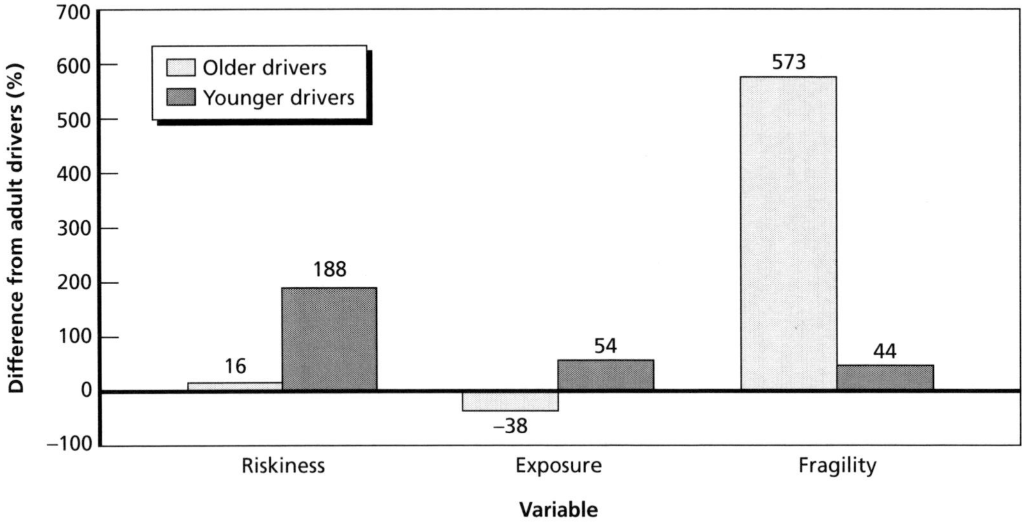

RAND *OP189-3.1*

## The Relative Fragility of Older Drivers

If older drivers are only slightly likelier to cause an accident than are adult drivers, then why do they appear to be at such a high risk of being in a fatal accident? The answer to this question can be found by examining the difference in the probability that older drivers will be killed in a crash. As illustrated in the third pair of bars in Figure 3.1, older drivers are 573 percent likelier to be killed in a crash than adult drivers are, while younger drivers are 44 percent likelier to be killed than adult drivers are.[1] We suspect, but cannot verify, that older drivers are also much likelier to sustain a nonfatal injury when involved in an accident.

## The Self-Regulation of Older Drivers

Our findings on the relative riskiness of older drivers are somewhat counterintuitive. Why, one might ask, do older drivers not appear riskier, given medical evidence that establishes that their driving skill declines with age? We propose that the answer is that older drivers change their driving habits to compensate for their diminished competence behind the wheel. Our analysis suggests that this self-regulation takes several forms.

First, many drivers simply cease driving at older ages because they pose an elevated risk to others and to themselves. The most dangerous drivers face pressure to stop driving from

---

[1] Technically speaking, the crash fatality rate we estimate is the likelihood that someone in type A's car dies relative to someone in type B's car. The reason this distinction is important is that the frequency with which one group drives with passengers, the average quality of a group's car, and differences in behavior (such as the propensity to wear seat belts) all play a key role. Thus, although younger drivers are not necessarily frailer than adult drivers, they may be likelier to drive unsafe cars or have passengers. With the case of older drivers, however, the difference is too large to be explained by any of these other factors.

a number of sources, including state regulations, family members, and their own survival instinct or self-interest. If older drivers are responsive to this pressure, then we might expect those at the greatest risk of causing an accident to remove themselves from the pool of drivers, leaving behind older drivers who drive comparatively well. Since our analysis is based on data about older drivers who continue to drive, our results will reflect this self-regulation.

Additional findings support this conjecture. Table 3.1 illustrates how our results change as we vary the group of drivers we define as *older* from 55 and older to 70 and older. As the group ages, the risk of being killed in a crash increases significantly, but the risk of causing a crash declines. In fact, the very oldest drivers are the *least* likely of all the four groups of older drivers to cause a crash—and half as likely as the group 55 and older. This result also defies conventional wisdom, which holds that the older the driver, the greater the risk that driver poses to other drivers. But it is consistent with the idea that the population of drivers becomes more competent with age because the worst drivers stop driving. Only the healthiest and safest older drivers remain on the road at very old ages.[2]

Second, our analysis offers evidence that older drivers avoid road conditions that put them at greater risk. For example, evidence suggests that, at advanced age, drivers find it more difficult to drive at rush hour and at night. If older drivers regulate their driving to promote safety, we would expect them to drive less during the peak daytime and nighttime hours. The results shown in Figure 3.2 confirm that assumption. Here, we plot changes in the exposure of older and younger drivers on the road at different times of day relative to their exposure at noon.[3] We present the results as relative to noon to control for the fact that exposure is mechanically higher for younger drivers (because there are more of them), so it is easier to compare the two series this way. Figure 3.2 shows that older drivers tend to stay off the road during peak traffic

**Table 3.1**
**Changes in the Relative Riskiness of Older Drivers for Different Definitions of *Older***

| Age Minimum to Be Considered Older (Years) | Increase Over Adult Drivers (%) | |
|---|---|---|
| | Relative Fragility | Relative Riskiness |
| 55 | 335 | 18 |
| 60 | 443 | 14 |
| 65 | 668 | 13 |
| 70 | 826 | 9 |

SOURCE: Loughran and Seabury (2007).

---

[2]  We should note that there are alternate explanations consistent with this finding. For instance, it could be that drivers become increasingly cautious and defensive as they age, so much so that they actually become safer drivers as they reach more advanced ages. But this is just a different kind of self-regulation.

[3]  Because older drivers tend to avoid the nighttime hours, we limit this analysis to the hours between 7:00 a.m. and 9:00 p.m. We exclude any crashes in which the FARS indicates that alcohol was a contributing factor and further restrict the sample to crashes occurring Monday through Friday, March through October, in areas with speed limits between 25 and 60 mph.

**Figure 3.2**
**Relative Exposure of Older and Younger Drivers, by Time of Day**

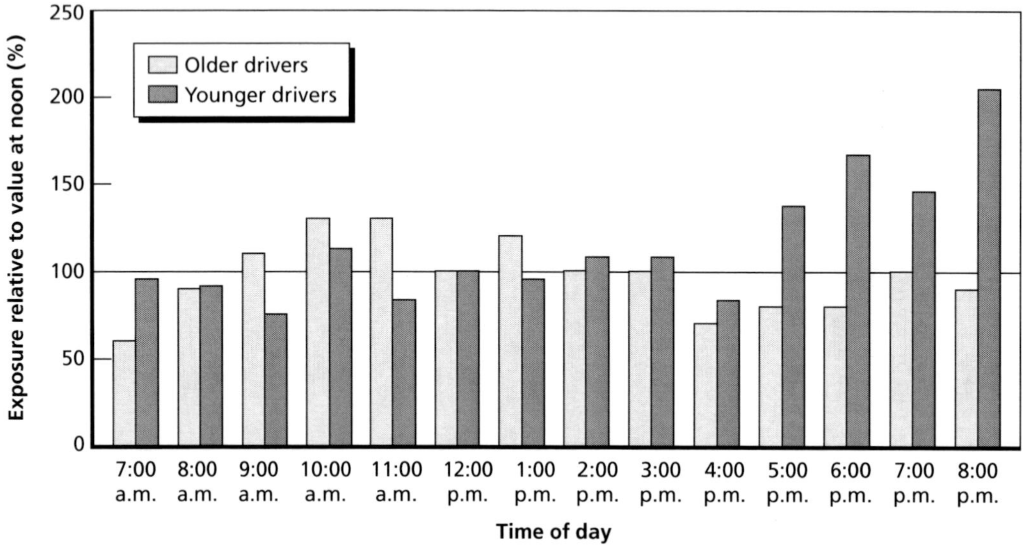

RAND *OP189-3.2*

times and appear most prevalent during off-peak daytime hours, particularly between 10:00 a.m. and noon. By contrast, younger drivers show no particular pattern during the day but drive more frequently at night.

## Summary of Findings

In summary, we find that older drivers are only slightly likelier than other drivers to cause an accident but are considerably likelier to be killed in one. Younger drivers, on the other hand, are considerably likelier than other drivers to cause a crash, drive much more frequently than older drivers, and are less susceptible to fatal injuries than older drivers are. These findings do not mean that driving skills do not, in fact, deteriorate with age as a result of worsening mental and physical impairments. Instead, our evidence suggests that older drivers adjust their behavior in light of these worsening impairments. Many older drivers cease to drive altogether; many others reduce the miles they drive and avoid the most dangerous driving conditions. Because they are aware of their own limitations and adjust their driving patterns in response, older drivers pose only a slightly increased risk to other drivers. The main danger they pose on the road is not to others but to themselves.

# CHAPTER FOUR

# Policy Implications

---

Given the physiological and cognitive changes that occur with age, it is natural for policymakers to be concerned about how the aging of the U.S. driving population will affect traffic safety. But just how concerned should policymakers be? In this final chapter, we examine the policy implications of our findings on the relative riskiness, exposure, and fragility of older drivers.

## The Role of Policy in Regulating Driver Safety

There are two reasons for the public to be concerned about older drivers: (1) the potential danger they pose to other drivers and passengers and (2) the danger they pose to themselves. Relatively stringent licensing policies for older drivers are more easily justified by the first concern than the second. The reason is that, as a society, we generally allow individuals more freedom to make choices that impose risks on themselves than we allow them to make choices that impose risks on others. Policy can be paternalistic, too, but usually more so when there is good reason to believe that individuals are making poorly informed choices about risk. In the case of driving, we might worry that older individuals suffer cognitive lapses that compromise their ability to evaluate their own competence as drivers. But we have no evidence that cognitive failure is the principal cause of poor driving ability in older individuals, and our evidence on self-regulation seems to imply that most older drivers make appropriate decisions about when to stop driving.

Now consider the first justification for stricter licensing requirements for older drivers. Suppose that an older individual is deciding whether to drive to the grocery store. We should expect that individual to weigh the costs and benefits of driving to the store versus other modes of transportation (e.g., walking, taking the bus). Importantly, the cost of driving to the grocery store includes the risk of getting into an accident and suffering an injury. Thus, older drivers, like all drivers, will account for their own likelihood of suffering injury (whether it be the result of their own or someone else's driving error) in deciding whether (or how much) to drive.

However, it is much less likely that the older individual, when deciding whether to drive, will fully account for the potential harm that he or she might inflict on other drivers and passengers, what we call the *social* cost of driving. In general, we expect driving to decline as the cost of driving increases. Thus, older drivers likely drive more than they would and more than is ideal from a societal perspective (or *socially optimal*) if they were to account for the possibility that they could harm not only themselves in an accident, but others, too. Of course, this problem is not unique to older drivers. It is likely that the vast majority of drivers, young and old, fail to account for the social cost of their decision to take a particular trip by car, which means that all drivers likely drive more than is socially optimal. But the degree to which a particular group of drivers drives too much increases with the likelihood that a member of that group will cause an accident. Our estimates indicate that older drivers are, in fact, likelier than adult drivers to cause an accident, which implies that older drivers exceed the socially optimal amount of driving for their group more than adult drivers do.

There are two general classes of policies that would help solve this problem: (1) directly limit the amount older individuals drive, and (2) raise the cost of driving so that older individuals have less of an incentive to drive. Both approaches have been taken in the case of drunk drivers, whose probability of causing an accident is vastly higher than that of sober drivers (see Levitt and Porter, 2001). Drunk driving is categorically prohibited, and the cost of drunk driving, if caught, is very high in terms of criminal and civil sanctions. Both types of policies are employed in the case of younger drivers as well, who we estimate to be nearly three times as likely to cause an accident as adult drivers. In many states, for example, teenage drivers cannot drive at night without an adult guardian present, and, in all states, insurers are allowed to charge significantly higher premiums for younger drivers.[1] More generally, poor driving, regardless of class, is punished via traffic citations and increases in insurance premiums (i.e., experience rating).

## Impact of Stricter Licensing Regulations

Does the relative riskiness of older drivers justify the same level of regulation as that imposed on drunk drivers and teenagers? Clearly not. Both drunk drivers and teenagers impose vastly higher risks than do older drivers. Levitt and Porter (2001) estimate that drunk drivers are seven to 13 times likelier than sober drivers to cause an accident, and, by our estimates, younger drivers are more than twice as likely as older drivers to cause an accident. Not only are teenagers likelier than older drivers to cause accidents, but they drive many more miles. As a result, drunk drivers and teenagers are responsible for many more traffic accidents each year than are older drivers.

In 2001, older drivers accounted for about 15 percent of all licensed drivers, and our estimates of relative riskiness and exposure imply that older drivers cause about 7 percent of all accidents. Thus, older drivers actually caused a small number of accidents relative to their proportion of licensed drivers. Younger drivers, on the other hand, cause 43 percent of all accidents, which is a disproportionately large percentage relative to their percentage of licensed drivers—13 percent in 2001.

By these measures, then, it would appear that older drivers actually pose no greater risk relative to their size of the population of licensed drivers than do adult drivers and certainly far

---

[1]   Insurance premiums affect the decision to drive (or the decision to purchase insurance) but generally not the amount one drives once one has decided to drive insured (Edlin, 2003).

less risk than do the youngest drivers. Thus, it is unclear from this evidence alone that licensing policies should target older drivers any more than they target adult drivers.

On the other hand, it could be that the licensing policies already in place are at least partly responsible for reducing the relative risk posed by older drivers today. That is, in the absence of such policies, older drivers as a group could be riskier than we observe them to be today. However, there is little empirical evidence to support this conjecture.

Evidence on the effect of licensing requirements on the accident rate of older drivers is limited and focused on vision testing. Some studies have found that states requiring vision tests for older drivers have lower older-driver fatal-accident rates (Levy, Vernick, and Howard, 1995; Shipp, 1999; Nelson, Sacks, and Chorba, 1992). Shipp (1999), for example, reports that the fatality rate is 12 percent lower among older drivers in states that require vision tests to obtain a driver's license than in states that do not. Grabowski, Campbell, and Morrisey (2004) do not find any evidence that vision testing affects the number of older-driver fatalities but do find evidence that in-person license renewals lower fatality rates among the oldest drivers (85 and older).

Our estimates indicate that the relative riskiness of older drivers changed little between the early 1970s and the last period of our data, 1998–2003, a time during which many states adopted stricter licensing requirements for older drivers (see Loughran and Seabury, 2007).

We have little doubt that more intensive screening would identify some older drivers whose licenses should be restricted or revoked entirely, perhaps leading to fewer tragic accidents like the one in Santa Monica, California, in 2003. But at what cost? DMVs would need to devote more resources to testing older drivers, and older drivers themselves would face the stress and stigma of being singled out because of their age. Moreover, we have no evidence that more intensive screening, if applied to all drivers, would be any likelier to identify particularly risky older drivers than it would be to identify particularly risky adult or younger drivers. Finally, there is the real possibility that screening of this sort would result in the premature termination of driving for some older drivers.

We do not suggest that screening programs targeting older drivers are inappropriate in all cases, but rather that the aggregate benefits in terms of improved traffic safety are likely to be small. In a number of states, for example, physicians are required to inform the DMV if they believe that a patient's driving ability may be impaired (e.g., if an older person is diagnosed with Alzheimer's disease). This requirement is likely to be relatively inexpensive to implement[2] and so may be justified even if relatively few traffic accidents are actually prevented as a result. Age-based road testing, on the other hand, is likely to be relatively expensive to implement, both in terms of DMV resources and the stigma older drivers might experience as a result of being singled out for this type of testing.[3]

We also note that we were unable to estimate the relative riskiness of the oldest drivers (e.g., 75 and older) using these methods. We do find that drivers 70 and older are no riskier than

---

[2]  The implication of such a policy for physician-patient confidentiality deserves careful consideration.

[3]  After receiving a barrage of complaints, the Council of the District of Columbia recently voted to prohibit the district's DMV from requiring drivers 75 and older to take a road test as a condition of license renewal. The DMV had just recently begun enforcing a decades-old municipal law allowing such road testing (see Karush, 2007).

those 65 and older, but it could be that relative riskiness climbs steeply at the most advanced ages. Even so, in formulating policy to address these oldest drivers, policymakers must take into account that there are very few of these drivers on the road, that self-regulation will likely succeed in removing many of the most dangerous older drivers, and that formulating licensing policies solely on the basis of age might be seen as discriminatory or otherwise unfair.

## Other Policy Recommendations

Our estimates imply that, as the U.S. population ages, the number of traffic accidents per capita could fall, although the seriousness of those accidents might increase. Although older drivers are somewhat likelier to cause an accident, they drive comparatively little, so overall, older drivers are only 13 percent as likely as adult drivers to cause an accident. Thus, an older driving population will mean fewer accidents per capita. But, since older drivers and passengers are so much likelier than other drivers and passengers to be killed in an accident, even as accidents per capita fall, fatalities per capita could rise. Given these trends, our research suggests that public policy should focus more on improving the safety of automobile travel for older drivers and less on screening out older drivers whose driving abilities have deteriorated unacceptably. Whatever benefits may be gained by imposing more rigid screening of older drivers could easily be outweighed by the costs of such policies to DMVs and older drivers themselves.

There are other types of policies that could help stem traffic-related fatalities as the U.S. population ages, although their cost-effectiveness would need to be evaluated. For example, policies should be considered that increase the safety of automobiles for older drivers in case of accidents. Automobile injury rates have fallen markedly over the past four decades, largely due to advances in automobile safety. Consumers will no doubt continue to demand advances in automobile safety in the coming years, and it seems likely that some of those advances will particularly benefit older drivers and passengers. For example, older individuals are likelier to suffer injuries due to seat belts and air-bag deployments. Advances in seat-belt and air-bag technologies that limit the force of these restraints could help reduce injuries among older individuals. In some instances, federal legislation has accelerated the rate at which safety innovations (e.g., seat belts) have permeated the automobile market. Federal policy could play a role in stimulating research into the causes of injuries sustained by older individuals in automobile accidents and perhaps mandating the adoption of feasible safety technologies when competitive forces appear to be inadequate in forcing their adoption.

Second, many states and associations (e.g., AAA and AARP) now offer older drivers voluntary, self-administered driving assessments or mature-driver courses. Although there is no scientific evidence that these tests and courses have been effective in reducing the riskiness of older drivers, these measures could be useful in helping older drivers and their families decide whether they should continue to drive and, if so, how much and under what conditions. Policies should be considered that foster the use of such instruments.

Finally, more public attention should be given to reducing the riskiness of younger drivers. Our analysis shows that younger drivers pose a much greater threat to the public than do drivers of any other age group. Because they drive so much more frequently and they cause such a high proportion of all accidents, reducing their riskiness by even a modest fraction would have far greater effect in terms of lives saved and injuries avoided than reducing the riskiness of older drivers by such a fraction.

# Bibliography

AARP, *The Policy Book: AARP Public Policies 2006*, Washington, D.C.: AARP, Legislative and Public Policy, 2006.

Augenstein, J., "Differences in Clinical Response Between the Young and Elderly," *Aging and Driving Symposium, Southfield, MI*, Des Plaines, Ill.: Association for the Advancement of Automotive Medicine, February 2001, pp. 19–20.

Baldock, M. R. J., J. L. Mathias, A. J. McLean, and A. Berndt, "Self-Regulation of Driving and Its Relationship to Driving Ability Among Older Adults," *Accident Analysis and Prevention*, Vol. 38, No. 5, September 2006, pp. 1038–1045.

Ball, Karlene K., Olivio J. Clay, Virginia G. Wadley, David L. Roth, Jerri D. Edwards, and Daniel L. Roenker, "Predicting Driving Performance in Older Adults with the Useful Field of View Test: A Meta-Analysis," *Proceedings of the Third International Driving Symposium on Human Factors in Driver Assessment, Training and Vehicle Design*, June 27–30, 2005, Rockport, Maine, pp. 51–57.

Davis, Robert, and Anthony DeBarros, "Older, Dangerous Drivers a Growing Problem," *USA Today*, May 2, 2007. As of May 2, 2007:
http://www.usatoday.com/news/nation/2007-05-02-older-drivers-usat1a_N.htm

Dellinger, Ann M., Jean A. Langlois, and Guohua Li, "Fatal Crashes Among Older Drivers: Decomposition of Rates into Contributing Factors," *American Journal of Epidemiology*, Vol. 155, No. 3, February 1, 2002, pp. 234–241.

Edlin, Aaron S., "Per-Mile Premiums for Auto Insurance," in Richard Arnott, Bruce Greenwald, Ravi Kanbur, and Barry Nalebuff, eds., *Economics for an Imperfect World: Essays in Honor of Joseph E. Stiglitz*, Cambridge, Mass.: MIT Press, 2003, pp. 53–82.

Evans, L., "Older Driver Involvement in Fatal and Severe Traffic Crashes," *Journal of Gerontology*, Vol. 43, No. 6, 1988, pp. S186–S193.

Evans, Leonard, and Peter H. Gerrish, "Gender and Age Influence on Fatality Risk from the Same Physical Impact Determined Using Two-Car Crashes," *SAE Transactions*, Vol. 110, No. 6, 2001, pp. 1336–1341.

Foley, Daniel J., Harley K. Heimovitz, Jack M. Guralnik, and Dwight B. Brock, "Driving Life Expectancy of Persons Aged 70 Years and Older in the United States," *American Journal of Public Health*, Vol. 92, No. 8, August 2002, pp. 1284–1289.

Grabowski, David C., Christine M. Campbell, and Michael A. Morrisey, "Elderly Licensure Laws and Motor Vehicle Fatalities," *Journal of the American Medical Association*, Vol. 291, No. 23, June 16, 2004, pp. 2840–2846.

Haas, Andrew L., "A Crash Course for the Elderly," *The New York Times*, July 17, 2006, p. A17.

IIHS—*see* Insurance Institute for Highway Safety.

III—*see* Insurance Information Institute.

Insurance Information Institute, "Older Drivers," May 2007. As of June 11, 2007:
http://www.iii.org/media/hottopics/insurance/olderdrivers/

Insurance Institute for Highway Safety, *Status Report*, Vol. 38, No. 3, March 15, 2003. As of June 11, 2007:
http://www.iihs.org/sr/pdfs/sr3803.pdf

————, "US Driver Licensing Procedures for Older Drivers," May 2007. As of June 11, 2007:
http://www.iihs.org/laws/state_laws/older_drivers.html

Jorgensen, Finn, and John Polak, "The Effect of Personal Characteristics on Drivers' Speed Selection: An Economic Approach," *Journal of Transport Economics and Policy*, Vol. 27, No. 3, September 1993, pp. 237–252.

Karush, Sarah, "Elderly Drivers Cry Foul in D.C.," *The Washington Times*, May 7, 2007, p. 1.

Kim, Karl, Lawrence Nitz, James Richardson, and Lei Li, "Personal and Behavioral Predictors of Automobile Crash and Injury Severity," *Accident Analysis and Prevention*, Vol. 27, No. 4, August 1995, pp. 469–481.

Kington, Raynard, David Reuben, Jeannette Rogowski, and Lee A. Lillard, *Health Status and Driving After Age 50*, Santa Monica, Calif.: RAND Corporation, DRU-318-NIA, 1993. As of January 7, 2007:
http://www.rand.org/pubs/drafts/DRU318/

Levitt, Steven D., and Jack Porter, "How Dangerous Are Drinking Drivers?" *The Journal of Political Economy*, Vol. 109, No. 6, December 2001, pp. 1198–1237. As of June 11, 2007:
http://www.journals.uchicago.edu/cgi-bin/resolve?JPE019605PDF

Levy, David T., Jon S. Vernick, and Kim Ammann Howard, "Relationship Between Driver's License Renewal Policies and Fatal Crashes Involving Drivers 70 Years or Older," *Journal of the American Medical Association*, Vol. 274, No. 13, October 4, 1995, pp. 1026–1030.

Li, Guohua, Elisa R. Braver, and Li-Hui Chen, "Fragility Versus Excessive Crash Involvement as Determinants of High Death Rates per Vehicle-Mile of Travel Among Older Drivers," *Accident Analysis and Prevention*, Vol. 35, No. 2, March 2003, pp. 227–235.

Loughran, David S., and Seth A. Seabury, *Estimating the Accident Risk of Older Drivers*, Santa Monica, Calif.: RAND Corporation, TR-450-ICJ, 2007.

Lyman, S., S. A. Ferguson, E. R. Braver, and A. F. Williams, "Older Driver Involvements in Police Reported Crashes and Fatal Crashes: Trends and Projections," *Injury Prevention*, Vol. 8, June 2002, pp. 116–120.

Marottoli, Richard A., Adrian M. Ostfeld, Susan S. Merrill, Gary D. Perlman, Daniel J. Foley, and Leo M. Cooney, Jr., "Driving Cessation and Changes in Mileage Driven Among Elderly Individuals," *Journal of Gerontology*, Vol. 48, No. 5, September 1993, pp. S255–S260.

Mendeloff, John, Christopher Nelson, Kilkon Ko, and Amelia Haviland, *Small Businesses and Workplace Fatality Risk: An Exploratory Analysis*, Santa Monica, Calif.: RAND Corporation, TR-371-ICJ, 2006. As of June 11, 2007:
http://www.rand.org/pubs/technical_reports/TR371/

"National Briefing: South: Florida: Victim of Driver, 93, Stuck in Windshield," *The New York Times*, October 22, 2005.

Nelson, D. E., J. J. Sacks, and T. I. Chorba, "Required Vision Testing for Older Drivers," *The New England Journal of Medicine*, Vol. 326, No. 26, June 25, 1992, pp. 1784–1785.

Ponds, R. W., W. H. Brouwer, and P. C. Van Wolffelaar, "Age Differences in Divided Attention in a Simulated Driving Task," *Journal of Gerontology*, Vol. 43, No. 6, 1988, pp. 151–156.

Shipp, M. D., "The Impact of State Vision-Testing Policies on Driving by Seniors," *Proceedings of the 15th Biennial Eye Research Seminar*, Los Angeles, Calif., September 26–29, 1999.

Stutts, Jane C., "Do Older Drivers with Visual and Cognitive Impairments Drive Less?" *Journal of the American Geriatrics Society*, Vol. 46, No. 1, 1998, pp. 854–861.

Tessmer, Joseph M., *FARS Analytic Reference Guide 1975–2002*, Washington, D.C.: U.S. Department of Transportation, National Highway Traffic Safety Administration, 2002.

Uc, E. Y., M. Rizzo, S. W. Anderson, Q. Shi, and J. D. Dawson, "Driver Route-Following and Safety Errors in Early Alzheimer Disease," *Neurology*, Vol. 63, No. 5, September 2004, pp. 832–837.

U.S. Public Roads Administration, U.S. Bureau of Public Roads, U.S. Federal Highway Administration, *Highway Statistics*, Washington, D.C.: Public Roads Administration, Federal Works Agency, annually since 1945. As of January 3, 2007:
http://purl.access.gpo.gov/GPO/LPS4717

Vance, David E., Daniel L. Roenker, Gayla M. Cissell, Jerri D. Edwards, Virginia G. Wadley, and Karlene K. Ball, "Predictors of Driving Exposure and Avoidance in a Field Study of Older Drivers from the State of Maryland," *Accident Analysis and Prevention*, Vol. 38, No. 4, July 2006, pp. 823–831.

Voelker, Rebecca, "Crash Risk Among Older Drivers Studied," *Journal of the American Medical Association*, Vol. 282, No. 17, November 3, 1999, pp. 1610–1611.

"Wrong Way: The D.C. Council Should Think Policy, Not Politics, in Deciding on Testing for Elderly Drivers," *The Washington Post*, June 5, 2007, p. A16.